Farming

Written by Ann Love with Jane Drake
Illustrated by Pat Cupples

Kids Can Press

"Thunderstorms are rolling our way," Dad calls. "Time to bring in the onions!"

"We'd better polish off lunch," Nick says to his cousin Karin. "There's work for us to do."

"But how can a little rain hurt onions?" Karin asks.

"Sometimes thunderstorms bring heavy rain and hail that can scar the onions we've left out on the field," Nick says. "People won't buy damaged onions, even for burgers."

"The best part of a burger is the beef, anyway." Karin grins. "Beef from a cattle ranch like ours."

"No way," Nick laughs. His family works together to operate a vegetable farm in Ohio, one of many different kinds of farms in the United States. Nick has helped to grow these onions since last winter. He knows getting them under cover is no joke.

3

Farmers in southern and some western states can plant vegetable seeds right in their fields in springtime. But where Nick lives, farmers must plant slow-growing vegetables like sweet onions and celery in greenhouses before the winter is over to give them a head start. Each seed is placed in a plug-tray and covered with moist soil and fertilizers specially mixed to help the plants grow.

Sun streams through the plastic windows of the greenhouse and heats the air and earth inside until everything feels summer warm. With daily watering, the seeds sprout and the plants start to grow. When the greenhouse cools down on wintry nights, backup heaters are turned on so the tender seedlings don't freeze.

As the spring days get warmer, farmers watch the greenhouse temperature. If it gets too hot for the young plants, they open the doors to let some of the heat escape.

4

Farmers count on machines to help them with their work. The tractor, with all its special attachments, is the most important machine on a vegetable farm.

When the ground is warming up in the spring, farmers prepare the soil for seeding and transplanting. Sometimes they use tractors with extra-wide tires in case there are still wet spots. No one wants to get stuck in the mud.

First, the tractor pulls a cultivator up and down the fields to loosen the soil with its long, sharp teeth. Then the disc and roller attachments break up, smooth and level the soil for seeding.

tractor with cultivator attachment

tractor with
disc attachment

roller attachment

7

Fast-growing vegetables like carrots and radishes can be seeded outside in April on Nick's farm. The seed drill sows six rows of seeds at once, at the proper distance apart and to the exact depth each vegetable requires.

tractor with seed drill

In early May when the weather is a little warmer, Nick's family moves the vegetable seedlings from their greenhouses to the fields. A special tractor attachment that seats five lets workers transplant seedlings five rows at a time, 120 plants a minute. Each young vegetable is given just enough space to grow to market size.

seedling transplanter

Most vegetable plants need lots of water when they are young, but some, like onions, need more later, when the bulb is swelling. If it doesn't rain, water can be pumped from a well or a river through plastic pipes to irrigate the crop.

Because weeds steal water, sunlight and food from vegetables, growers pull any weeds they see and carry them off the field. Through the summer, farmers regularly dig and turn the soil between rows to stop weeds from rooting and to allow water to soak in.

water sprinkler

10

Farmers watch their crops carefully for signs of disease and for insects that may cause damage. They can fight disease and pests by spraying the plants with chemicals. Nick's family prefers to use environmentally friendly ways to protect the crops. That's why they grow several kinds of vegetables and rotate them to different fields each year. So when pests that like onions return to the field where they found onions last year, they find carrots or celery instead.

Vegetables ripen at different times. On Nick's farm, the onions are ready by midsummer when the green tops of the plants flop over and the outer skin of the bulb dries. When the soil is wet, onion farmers attach an onion windrower to their tractors. It digs out the bulbs, knocks off the soil, and lays the onions back on top of the field to dry in the sun.

onion windrower

After ten days of drying, the farmers use an onion harvester to lift the onions from the field and shake them gently up a conveyer belt to loosen any remaining dirt. Some harvesters sort and pack the onions using machines. Others need workers to stand at a sorting table, twist off leftover leaves and put aside damaged bulbs before the good ones are hand-packed into wooden pallet boxes. Plastic is stretched over the tops of filled onion boxes to keep out rain and hail.

tractor with
onion harvester

On Nick's farm, the boxes sit on the fields until September and the onions keep on drying. Then the boxes are moved into storage sheds that have fans to suck in the cool night air. The onions are kept cool and dry so they will stay alive and crisp for many months.

Farmers work hard so they can get good prices for their vegetables. If they can keep their crop fresh, grocers and food processors will pay better prices.

Once all the onions are boxed, everyone can relax.

"Cows must be easy to farm," Nick teases. "They just chew grass until they're ready for market."

"No," Karin shakes her head. "When you visit our ranch next summer, we'll work as hard as we did today."

"I can take that," Nick says, "but I'll bring my own veggies to fix a decent burger when we're through!"

"It's a deal!" Karin laughs. "And we'll serve you the best beef patty you've ever tasted."

15

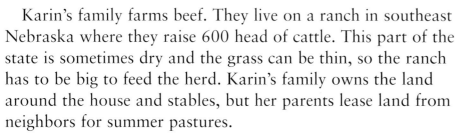

Karin's family farms beef. They live on a ranch in southeast Nebraska where they raise 600 head of cattle. This part of the state is sometimes dry and the grass can be thin, so the ranch has to be big to feed the herd. Karin's family owns the land around the house and stables, but her parents lease land from neighbors for summer pastures.

It doesn't take long for the herd to chew down the grass in a large meadow. About once a week, all summer, the cowhands have to round up the cattle and drive them along wooded trails and around wetlands to fresher pastures.

When Nick arrives, everyone is getting ready for a cattle drive. They have to move the cattle about 5 miles early the next day before it gets hot and the cows grow tired.

17

On a cattle drive, cowhands ride their horses behind the main herd, forcing the cattle forward. It's a noisy, dusty job. The cows and their calves moo constantly. The cowhands use their dogs to help round up any cattle that wander off the trail. They shout "Watch her, watch her, bring her back!" to the cow dogs, who then bark and chase the strays back. Frisky bulls push one another around and stir up dirt in the middle of the herd, but the cattle keep moving slowly forward.

Finally the herd reaches the new pasture and the cowhands stop, relax and listen. When the mooing quiets down, they know each cow has claimed her calf. Only then can the tired cowhands ride back to the ranch house.

Summer is also the time to grow hay for the cows' winter feed. Karin's family sows alfalfa on fields close to a stream or wetland. In dry spells, they water their crop. Three or four times each summer they cut the hay, lay it on the fields to dry in the sun, and then bale and store it until winter. If they grow more hay than they need, her family will sell the extra hay to feed cattle in other parts of the country.

wheeled irrigation pipes

hay baler

cattle
guard

post driver

Hayfields are fenced to keep cattle and horses out, and every summer the fences have to be repaired or replaced. The ranch tractor has an attachment for pounding in the posts. Cowhands wear gloves to string barbed wire. They tighten the wire with a tool called a hand winch.

Where a road enters a fenced-off field, ranchers don't always use swing gates. Instead they lay pipes into the road. Cows and horses refuse to cross the pipes, but ranchers can drive over these cattle guards, or Texas gates, without having to stop and open and then stop and shut gates.

In the fall, the cattle are rounded up one last time and driven close to the ranch buildings.

Most of the calves are big enough to sell. Some are trucked straight from the roundup to a meatpacking plant, where they are butchered. Many are sold to farmers who will fatten them up and slaughter them later. A few of the strongest female calves are auctioned off to ranchers who will add them to their herds. Ranchers work hard all year long to find the best prices for their livestock.

The herd lives outside all winter, corralled in the hayfields away from the biting wind. Pregnant cows get the most sheltered fields beside the house. Bulls are separated from all the others and kept in their own corral.

23

The herd is much smaller after the fall market, but in February new calves are born and the herd grows again. Everyone on the ranch takes turns checking on the pregnant cows day and night. A cow may need help with a birth, or a newborn calf may need dry straw to lie on.

Young calves spend most of the time sleeping. When they want their mothers, they don't go looking, they just stand up and bawl. Each mother recognizes her calf's special cry and comes to offer milk.

In late spring, the calves are branded with the sign of their ranch so they can be identified and returned if they wander away. Some ranchers use ear tags. On Karin's farm, an iron brand, heated in a bonfire, burns the sign onto the calf's thick-skinned rump, where it will hurt the least. At the same time, veterinarians vaccinate the calves against disease and cut out their horn buds so they won't harm one another when they butt heads. Everyone works quickly to get the calves back to their mothers.

Neighbors help one another out on branding days because it's a big job on every ranch. When the work is done, everyone catches up on the news and enjoys a meal around the bonfire.

After branding, the herd is moved to its summer pasture. The cowhands check on the cattle every day. When they see that the grass is grazed low, they know it's time to drive the herd to a fresh meadow again.

It takes all morning for the cowhands and their dogs to drive the cattle to their new pasture. Nick and Karin are stiff, tired and hungry when they get back to the house.

"I need an extra-thick burger," Nick says. "After all that riding, I'm hungry."

Karin grins. "I'll need at least two of your crispy onion slices on mine and lots of fresh lettuce."

"It's a cross-country job just to make a burger," Nick says, and they both laugh.

29

Nick and Karin's Cross-Country Lunch

There are different kinds of farms in every state. Nick's and Karin's family farms represent two main kinds of agriculture — growing plants and raising animals. The ingredients of this American hamburger lunch come from right across the country.

The bun is made from flour that comes from wheat grown on a farm in sunny Kansas.

The cheese is made with milk taken from dairy cows that eat the sweet grass in Wisconsin. The milk in the glass comes from a dairy farm too.

The lettuce was grown on a vegetable farm in California, the onion grew in Ohio and the tomato ripened in Florida.

The beef patty comes from a cow raised on a cattle ranch in Nebraska.

The potato salad is made from potatoes grown in the good soil of Idaho.

The peaches and cherries were grown in fruit orchards in South Carolina, Georgia and Oregon.

Index

alfalfa, 20

beef, 2, 16, 30
branding, 26
bulls, 18, 22

California, 30
calves, 18–19, 22, 24, 26
cattle, 2, 16–19, 21, 22–27, 30
cattle drives, 16, 18–19, 27, 28
cattle guards, 21
cattle ranching, 16–28, 30
chemicals, 11
cow dogs, 18, 28
cowhands, 16, 18, 19, 21, 27, 28
cows, 18–19, 22, 24, 30.
   See also cattle

dairy cows, 30
diseases, 11, 26

environmental concerns, 11

fall, 14, 22, 24
fences, 21
fertilizers, 4
fields, 6–14, 20, 21, 22
Florida, 30

fruit, 30

Georgia, 30
grass, 16, 27
greenhouses, 4, 9

harvesting, 12–14, 20
hay, 20, 21, 22
herds, 16, 18–19, 22, 24, 27
horns, 26

Idaho, 30
insects, 11

Kansas, 30

machinery, 6, 8, 9, 10, 12, 13, 20, 21
markets, 9, 14, 22, 24
meatpacking plants, 22
milk, 24, 30

Nebraska, 16, 30

onions, 2, 4, 10–14, 30
Ohio, 2, 30
Oregon, 30

pastures, 16, 19, 27

planting, 4, 8, 9, 20

rain, 2, 10, 13
rotation, crops, 11
roundups, 16, 22

seeding, 4, 6, 8
seedlings, 4, 9
soil, 4, 6, 10, 12, 13
South Carolina, 30
spring, 4, 6, 8, 9, 26
summer, 4, 10, 12, 16, 20, 21, 27
sun, 4, 12, 20

tractors, 6–7, 8, 9, 12, 13, 14, 20, 21
transplanting, 6, 9

vegetable farming, 2–14, 30
vegetables, 2–14, 30
veterinarians, 26

water, 4, 10, 20
weather, 2, 10
weeds, 10
wheat, 30
winter, 4, 14, 20, 22, 24
Wisconsin, 30

This book is dedicated to Andrea, Brianna, Natalie, Hilary, Judy and Ian.
With thanks — A.L.

The authors gratefully acknowledge the assistance of Kathleen and Henry Barnett; Jeff Chisholm; Ellis Greenstein; Bart Hall; Christy, Jane, Mark, Kathleen and Bob Haywood-Farmer; Betty and Gage Love; Melanie, Jennifer, Adrian and David Love; Mary Ruth McDonald; Maire Ullrich; and, of course, the Little Red Hen.

Thank you to Valerie Hussey, Ricky Englander and all the people at Kids Can Press. Thanks to Pat Cupples, whose illustrations enliven the pages with authenticity and humor. And special thanks to Debbie Rogosin and Lynda Prince for their care for detail and warm encouragement.

First U.S. edition 1998

Text © 1996 Ann Love and Jane Drake
Illustrations © 1996 Pat Cupples

Published in Canada by
Kids Can Press Ltd.
29 Birch Avenue
Toronto, ON M4V 1E2

Published in the U.S. by
Kids Can Press Ltd.
2250 Military Road
Tonawanda, NY 14150

www.kidscanpress.com

The artwork in this book was rendered in watercolor, gouache, graphite and colored pencil on hot-press watercolor paper.

Edited by Debbie Rogosin
Designed by Marie Bartholomew and Karen Powers
Printed in China

The hardcover edition of this book is smyth sewn casebound. The paperback edition of this book is limp sewn with a drawn-on cover.

US 98 0 9 8 7 6 5 4 3 2 1
US PA 02 0 9 8 7 6 5 4 3 2 1

National Library of Canada Cataloguing in Publication Data

Love, Ann
     Farming

(America at work)
Includes index.
ISBN 1-55074-451-8 (bound).   ISBN 1-55337-421-5 (pbk.)

     1. Agriculture — United States — Juvenile literature.
I. Drake, Jane II. Cupples, Patricia III. Title. IV. Series:
America at work (Toronto, Ont.)

S519.L68 1998   j630'.973   C98-930319-5

Kids Can Press is a  Entertainment company